Christmas
by Design

Schiffer Publishing

Other Schiffer Books by the Authors:
Christmas at Designers' Homes across America, ISBN: 978-0-7643-5163-1

Library of Congress Control Number: 2018937447

Designed by Molly Shields
Cover design by RoS
Cover photo: Dan Piassick, courtesy IBB Design

Type set in Aphrodite Slim Stylistic/ ZapfEllipt

ISBN: 978-0-7643-5654-4
Printed in China

Published by Schiffer Publishing, Ltd.
4880 Lower Valley Road
Atglen, PA 19310
Phone: (610) 593-1777; Fax: (610) 593-2002
E-mail: Info@schifferbooks.com
Web: www.schifferbooks.com

For our complete selection of fine books on this and related subjects, please visit our website at www.schifferbooks.com. You may also write for a free catalog.

Schiffer Publishing's titles are available at special discounts for bulk purchases for sales promotions or premiums. Special editions, including personalized covers, corporate imprints, and excerpts, can be created in large quantities for special needs. For more information, contact the publisher.

We are always looking for people to write books on new and related subjects. If you have an idea for a book, please contact us at proposals@schifferbooks.com.

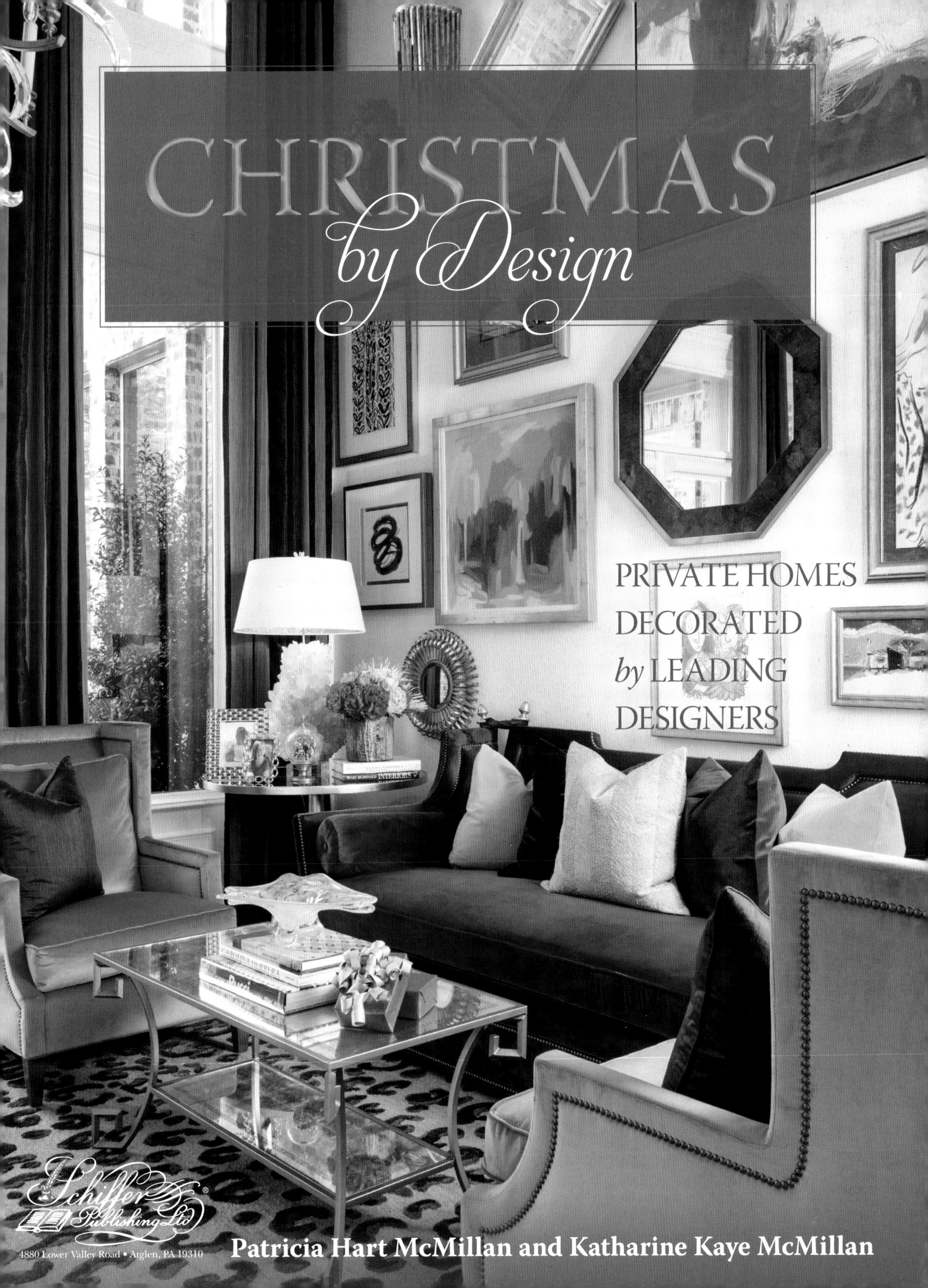

CHRISTMAS
by Design

PRIVATE HOMES
DECORATED
by LEADING
DESIGNERS

Schiffer
Publishing Ltd

4880 Lower Valley Road • Atglen, PA 19310

Patricia Hart McMillan and Katharine Kaye McMillan

to Jesus, the Christ

Fear not, for behold, I bring you good tidings of great joy,

which shall be to all people.

—Luke 2:10, KJV

CONTENTS

9 *Foreword*   10 *Foreword*   11 *Acknowledgments*   12 *Introduction*

14 **Mediterranean**
Hunter House,
Scottsdale, Arizona

24 **Color**
City Home,
McLean, Virginia

32 **Magic**
Garcia Residence,
San Antonio, Texas

38 **Glamour**
Traditional Home,
Little Rock, Arkansas

44 **Romance**
Webb Residence,
Atlanta, Georgia

50 **Candyland**
Howard Residence,
San Antonio, Texas

56 **Treasures**
Hanley Residence,
Scottsdale, Arizona

70 **Cozy**
Gawlik Residence,
Scottsdale, Arizona

86 **Feliz**
Gallagher Ranch,
San Antonio, Texas

94 **Funfetti**
Geyer Residence,
Frisco, Texas

112 **Tannenbaum**
Galt Residence,
Brookhaven, Georgia

118 **Tradition**
Labatt Residence,
San Antonio, Texas

128 **Joy**
Beach Residence,
Wichita, Kansas

132 **Classic**
Lightfoot House at Colonial Williamsburg,
Williamsburg, Virginia

136 **Love**
Stith Residence,
San Antonio, Texas

144 **Retro**
Plantation Residence,
Adel, Georgia

150 **Victorian**
Vollmer Residence,
Brentwood, Tennessee

156 **Neo-Classical**
Stone Residence,
San Antonio, Texas

166 **Green**
Storey Residence,
Marks, Mississippi

178 **Natural**
Eddington Residence,
Little Rock, Arkansas

188   **Nostalgic**
Little Cottage,
San Antonio, Texas

194   **Gilded**
Atlanta Homes & Lifestyles Show House,
Atlanta, Georgia

198   **Tropical**
Contemporary Residence,
West Palm Beach, Florida

208   **Fairyland**
Tips Residence,
San Antonio, Texas

218   **Country**
Stonesthrow,
St. Louis, Missouri

230   **Collectible**
Parker and d'Andrimont Residence,
Lakewood, Colorado

236   **Moorish**
Anzoategui Residence
San Antonio, Texas

240   **Merry**
McClure Residence,
Wilmington, North Carolina

246   **Glorious**
Blalock Residence,
Arlington, Virginia

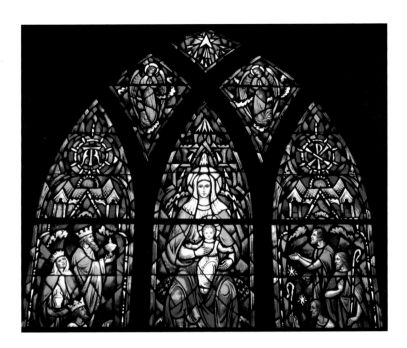

FOREWORD

Christmas, Home, and Heart

How often we talk about our dream home as a place we inhabited in the past or one we idealize in our future. For me, "dream home" conjures a vision of our French country clapboard house, set in the foothills of the Appalachians, where we lived when our three children were young. My imagination takes me back to that place quite often as a sort of Eden, because I conveniently forget the incessant problems with the well, and the long afternoons chopping firewood and clearing snow.

As a pastor of thirty years, I know the real dreamer of home was Joseph of the Holy Family. Four times he is given dreams by God's angels to secure the Christ child's future. First, he is commended to take the disgraced Mary as his wife. Second, he is warned of Herod's determination to execute the infant Jesus, and told to flee to Egypt. In Joseph's third and fourth dreams, he is assured they can return from Egypt to Nazareth to establish the home where Jesus will be reared in the embrace of Mary and Joseph (Matthew 1:20–21; 2:13; 2:19–20, 2:22).

Photograph by Susanna Kitayama.

Joseph reminds us that our abodes are not special because they have a double convection oven or a Tiffany chandelier or even a lap pool or Jacuzzi. No, those houses that inhabit our memories or catalyze our fantasies are not special because of the appliances, accoutrements, or bright furniture we add to them, but because of the people with whom we share them and the life we build within them. After all, about the same time Jesus was walking the Earth, Pliny the Elder (23–79 AD), a Roman soldier turned philosopher, said, "Home is where the heart is."

—William Patrick Gahan III, Rector, Christ Episcopal Church, San Antonio, The Third Sunday of Advent

FOREWORD

Homes for Holidays

I have been blessed to have designed more than a thousand homes in my thirty-five-year career. So much inspiration, collaboration, and plain hard work go into the creation of these homes, which are beautiful in their own right 365 days a year. But nothing is more rewarding than seeing them adorned for Christmas. I marvel at the level of detail and customization my clients infuse into their homes at this delightful time of year. In some cases, the residences are larger than 10,000 square feet, yet virtually every room has some level of holiday decoration that imparts meaning, memory, or sentiment. Their homes speak of their love for capturing the memories, history, and delight of Christmastime.

For architectural and interior designers, it is a reminder that these are our clients' homes. We are merely there to assist in orchestrating and choreographing their visions. Decorating one's home for the holidays is a uniquely personal effort. I hope you enjoy this beautiful book and that it inspires you to build on your own family's history and memories as you celebrate this festive season.

—Mark Candelaria, AIA, Candelaria Design, Scottsdale, Arizona

Architect Mark Candelaria, left, with clients Laurie and Jonathan Hunter (top right), Nancy Hanley (top left), and Robert and Mary Ellen Gawlik (bottom right). He designed their homes with entertaining in mind.

ACKNOWLEDGMENTS

Our gratitude goes to publisher Pete Schiffer for his enthusiastic support, and to Cheryl Weber, our excellent editor.

Photograph by Cody Deer, courtesy Debby Gromulka Designs

INTRODUCTION

The Joy of Design

Christmas, a season of unrestrained joy, is the one time of the year for decorating with passion—perhaps even abandon! It's a time for pulling out all the stops, going over the edge, "jingling your bells," as Palm Beach designer Keith Carrington says. It's a time for being "as tacky as we like," adds Florida interior designer Cecil Hayes (an *Architectural Digest* "Top 100" designer). But even with license to commit decorating *faux pas*, most of us appreciate some guidelines. And even we professionals are on the lookout for inspiration. Seeing how others—especially professional designers—express themselves can be helpful. Since design is design (essential aesthetic rules are the same for any design field), we bring you interiors by architectural, interior, landscape, floral, and decorative accessories designers—and a few gifted homeowner-designers who may (or may not) work with professionals. Katharine and I hope you find all their designs and our book a boon to your own joyful Christmas decorating.
　　—Patricia Hart McMillan

Photography by Dan Piassick,
courtesy IBB Design

Mediterranean

Hunter House,
Scottsdale, Arizona
Mark Candelaria, architect

Christmas wreaths on elegant iron gates welcome guests to Jonathan and Laurie Hunter's home for the holidays. Laurie leaves the two large glass double front doors free of decoration so as not to obstruct the visitor's view of the entry's nine-foot tree and gorgeous cedar garland adorned with blue-gray berries. The tree, with platinum and gold ornaments, hints at the excitement to come, and the entry stairs keep that promise. "Decorating my stairs and fireplaces is a must," says Laurie. "I lavish them with garlands of an assortment of winter greenery and magnolia, along with tons of heavy, wired velvet ribbon. I like the gold accents for the dramatic effect."

A traditionalist, Laurie says her style is "dressy and formal." Her decorating concept starts with choosing a theme and colors. "I tend to do a lot of gold tones mixed with other colors," she says. "One tree is usually in gold tones. Another will mix gold and burgundy. A third tree carries the gold theme and mixes in pops of silver, which ties all the trees together. Some of my ornaments I have collected over the years; others I've acquired more recently. I love them all."

Two of the three trees are artificial. "We include a real tree for its traditional Christmas fragrance," she says. "In the main room is the special dressy tree—the first thing that I plan in detail." It is festooned with velvet ribbon and jewel-like ornaments, and its pine cones are gold-dipped for added sparkle.

On the mantel, Hunter goes "big and dressy, making a dramatic statement." Throughout the house are candles, flowers, and fresh sprigs of cedar to dress the tables, which adds a wonderful festive fragrance.

A favorite of the couple and their four children is the nutcracker collection prominently displayed in the kitchen—more than forty in all shapes and sizes, each with a different story behind them.

Their architect, Mark Candelaria, says the firm's designs always plan for an exterior and interior Christmas scenario. "The holiday décor of this home far surpasses anything I envisioned," he adds.

Guests arriving at double glass doors are treated to views of the beribboned stair and Christmas tree.

Jonathan and Laurie Hunter greet guests in the living room, presided over by a magnificent Christmas tree (and sometimes watched over by a beloved guard dog).

Photography by Julianne Palmer, Pearl Blossom Photography, courtesy Candelaria Design

Garlands above the stove, decorations on the counter, and a hutch full of nutcrackers enliven the kitchen.

Garland for the chandelier looks fresh and lovely in the simply decorated breakfast room.

The dining room is deftly decorated with a charming centerpiece for the dining table.

Nativity figurines of Joseph, Mary, and the Christ child adorn a marble-topped chest.

Poinsettias enhance the patio.

The Hunters' home was designed with entertaining in mind. Scalloped swags of simple, elegant garland welcome holiday guests.

Color

City Home,
McLean, Virginia
Mary Douglas Drysdale, interior designer

"Christmas should always be upbeat, and should be about remembering those who have helped us along the way," says interior designer Mary Douglas Drysdale.

Known for her adroit use of color in interiors that have appeared in *Traditional Home, House Beautiful, Architectural Digest,* and a host of other decorating magazines, Drysdale says, "I plan my Christmas decorating schemes—although I may deviate once I get started. The first thing I plan for is color—I like to work with color themes. The choice depends on my mood. Any color works for me, as long as it is pretty in the application."

If her colors are upbeat, they may also be offbeat. For example, she strings a Japanese tree in the garden with pink lights that accentuate its delicate branches. Once, she decorated an entire tree with burned-out light bulbs painted in pretty colors. Another tree was hung with animal-farm cookies "frosted in fun Christmasy colors."

And while nothing can compare with the fragrance of a real tree, she doesn't always have the time to decorate a big tree. "When a big tree is out, I don't mind a small tabletop faux tree, which is festive but not pretending to be something it is not." Glamorous yet down-to-earth, Mary adds, "I used to swag the stairs, but I have become much more practical. The pine needles and sticky stuff have me now leaving the stairs alone."

Interior designer Mary Douglas Drysdale dons a Santa hat. *Photography by Ron Blunt, courtesy Drysdale, Inc.*

Mary remodeled and decorated a client's McLean, Virginia, house. Relocating a staircase created an impressive two-story entry with walls newly covered in antique-look Venetian plaster. On a chair back a wreath waits to be hung.

The new entry provides an expanded view into the inviting family room.

Five men hoisted the giant tree into place in the family room with a color scheme keyed to the Oushak rug from Stark Carpet. A huge Sam Gilliam painting adds a modern note. New rear windows and French doors are visible from the entry.

An American quilt adds punchy color and pattern to the kitchen, with its blue-gray walls and cabinets. Christmas greenery and a wreath add seasonal zest.

The formal living room is enlivened with Mary's favorite mix—antique furniture and contemporary art. Beautifully wrapped Christmas gifts add a decorative note. Atop the packages are painted burnt-out light bulb ornaments.

Draperies in a Scalamandre green plaid led design decisions in the dining room. Oranges, a holiday treat in Colonial days, and a bowl of colorful ornaments decorate the expansion dining table surrounded by French chairs.

A stylishly dressed mannequin *cum* Christmas tree and beautifully wrapped Christmas presents decorate the master bedroom, with its romantic four-poster French bed. On the floor is a contemporary interpretation of a Romanian oriental rug in pale green with deep blue patterns.

Magic

Garcia Residence,
San Antonio, Texas
Cheri Stith and Jamie Weyand, Christmas décor

Amy Garcia and her husband moved into their 1960s Tudor-style house five months before Christmas, after working with designer Raven Labatte to update the interiors. The weekend after Thanksgiving, she hired Cheri Stith and Jamie Weyand, owners of the local Feather, Fluff & Flings, to help her decorate for Christmas. Outside, the pair hung lavish garlands embellished with colorful ribbon and seasonal berries. Inside they focused on the entry stair banister, fireplace mantels, and Christmas trees.

"For the first time, we decorated two trees, each in a different style," Amy says. "While I love the fragrance and feel of a real tree, my practical side got the better of me. I wanted to start fresh with décor that I can build on each year, so we purchased artificial trees."

The tree in the mid-century-style living room reflects the period with its black-and-white color scheme. The white tree is decorated with black, white, and gold ornaments and ribbon, with a splash of red for drama. The more traditional family room tree features bright reds and greens.

The Garcia family's annual traditions include caroling in the neighborhood with friends and their children, attending a Nutcracker performance, and donating their time to various charity events.

"What makes Christmas special for us are all the normal things—leaving cookies and milk out for Santa, remembering to move the darn Elf-on-the-Shelf every night, sending and receiving Christmas cards, and all the magical things that my children experience," Amy says. "To see the joy and excitement through your children's eyes is truly the most special thing about the holiday season."

Beribboned garlands welcome visitors to the Garcia's Elmcourt home. Photography by Natalia Sun

Colorful garland frames the graceful entry hall stair.

Bold red ribbon on the Christmas tree and mantel garland counterpoint the living room's black-and-white scheme.

Traditional red-and-green decorations
enliven the great room.

A jolly elf sits in a bowl of shiny ornaments
on the kitchen counter.

Glamour

Traditional Home,
Little Rock, Arkansas
Shayla Copas, Christmas décor

Not every designer buys the less-is-more mantra. "You can never overdo Christmas," says Shayla Copas, who designs interiors for high-profile clients. "For me it's always more, especially when I'm decorating a mantel. Still, focus should always be on the tree, even in rooms with mantels."

While her firm designs both traditional and contemporary projects, she loves a traditional holiday design. "You can never go wrong with a red, green, and gold color scheme," she says.

For this project, Shayla sat down with her client to discover what her dream Christmas would look like. "For this very special client, who loves jewel tones, we added blue and purple to a palette of red, green, and gold. Since red is her favorite color, we emphasized the red."

Traditional design need never be dull. "My client and I both love glam, glam, and more glam," she says. "My mantra is everything that sparkles. Sparkle adds a sense of movement and life to interiors." So what should her style be called? "Glam traditional," she says.

Interior designer Shayla Copas.

Shayla Copas decorates stairs with flair, emphasizing elegant lines. *Photography by Janet Warlick, courtesy Shayla Copas Interiors*

Similar ornaments for the mantel garland and tree decorations create a sense of harmony. Gift wrappings restate the scheme.

Crystal adds sparkle to the coffee table.

On the dining table, greenery adorned with jewel-like ornaments create a setting for baroque sculptures and a Renaissance angel.

A second tree is trimmed in traditional red and green; a third reflects a passion for purple.

Shayla Copas believes that a master bedroom deserves a magnificently decorated mantel and a glorious tree.

Romance

Webb Residence,
Atlanta, Georgia
Beth Webb, interior designer

Christmas for award-winning designer Beth Webb is not always in December. Working with magazines often means designing a photo shoot concept far ahead of the holiday season. The year she designed a Christmas photo shoot in August, there was no garland to be had. "We had to make our own—outside, in August, in Atlanta!" she says. Beth describes her style as "simply elegant for both town and country homes." "In the city I am absolutely chicer than in the country—china, fine linens, crystal, gold and silver for the dinner table. Last Christmas, décor was gold and white for the city. In the country I can indulge my rustic side, so our low-country glass house on the marsh was a birch bark affair."

"Over the years," Beth says, "I've probably done more transitional-style decorating. But of late I find I am increasingly tailored, much more edited in my approach. I think that has as much to do with my aesthetic sensibilities as with time-management issues.

"We are all just so busy these days; still designers all want to do something new and different," she continues. "Unfortunately for my children, every year brought something different in the way of holiday décor at home. When they were small, we had all the blown-glass ornaments and the remnants of all we'd grown up with from my mother and grandmother. Every year getting them out was a trip down memory lane. Then I began collecting

mercury glass. Lately, if I find something unusual while traveling or shopping for clients, it becomes the year's focal point."

In her Atlanta home the living room mantel has always been the focal point. "Whether it is a garland or just cut greenery, the mantel is always dressed for the holidays," says Beth. "Our choice of mantels to install in clients' homes is often dictated by just that very thing. They want at least a five-inch-wide mantel for Christmas décor." The server is often the focal point in Beth's dining room. "I stack gobs of beautifully decorated gifts on top and underneath."

When it comes to decorating for Christmas, Beth says she's done it all. Well, almost all. She remembers an image that TV

personality Clinton Smith sent her of a stair somewhere in Northern Europe. Spilling all the way down the stone stairs were candles surrounded by hundreds of gold glass ornaments. "I don't have the stone stair, or the ornaments, but I've always wanted to recreate that," she says. Her most memorable photo shoot featured meringue Christmas trees. "A friend made them for me, and I've never grown tired of those images," she says.

Beth says her greatest holiday treat is being invited to Elway Hall, the home of her friend Barry Dixon. "Every single room is decorated to the nines and almost every room has its own tree," she says. "The fires are laid in each hearth, and there are fresh flowers in every single room. Candles run the length of each hall. Elway Hall is absolutely the most romantic setting you will have ever seen! I'd like to just go there every year."

Another perfect Christmas holiday destination is Blackberry Farm in Tennessee. "I'm from Tennessee, and my husband and I were married at Blackberry Farm on December 2," she says. "I've had a very long love affair with that property. It's the perfect place for Christmas and all that the season brings."

Designer Beth Webb trims her fireplace in gracefully hung garlands of the utmost simplicity. *Photography by Erica George Dines, courtesy Beth Webb Interiors*

Beth Webb at home.

Wooden acorn sculptures nest in a bed of greenery.

A wreath of white berried greenery hangs above meringue Christmas-tree sculptures, gifts from a friend.

An elegant silver epergne reigns over a table laden with sweet treats.

Beth "is chicer" in the city, setting her tables with fine china, crystal, silver, and monogrammed linens.

Candyland

Howard Residence,
San Antonio, Texas
Cherie Stith and Jamie Weyand, Christmas décor

Luxuriously decorated double doors create a joyous welcome to Mike and Meredith Howard's home at Christmastime. Those handsome doors open into a spacious hallway that extends the length of the house. Immediately to the left is an inviting sitting room with matching, rosy-red sofas facing one another across a coffee table. "I love this room," says Meredith, who owns M2H Communications, a public relations firm. "My grandmother had a saying: 'If you like it, it goes.' I have really taken that to heart. We don't do matchy-matchy. All the décor in our home—year-round and during the holidays—represents places we've been, people we've met, and experiences we've shared as a family."

Mike and Meredith have three children: Jaden, fourteen; Jack, four; and two-year-old Adele Margaret. "When thinking about Christmas décor, I wanted something whimsical, fun, and not too formal," Meredith says. She hired Feather, Fluff & Flings to create bright, Candyland-esque elements that would resonate with her young children.

The whimsical living room Christmas tree featured pinks, turquoise, purples, yellow, and lime-green ornaments and decorations, while the family room tree contained reds and greens and was embellished with snowflakes. A special "family" tree was reserved for treasured ornaments from the couple's childhood and their children's homemade ornaments. "Nothing about this tree is formal or matches," Meredith says. "It is our memory tree."

While parties and dinners are all part of the festivities, "what we love to do is drive around with our little ones and look at Christmas lights," she says.

The Howard family greet holiday guests to their joyously decorated home. *Photography by Natalia Sun*

Meredith Howard reads a Christmas story to Jack in front of the gaily decorated family room fireplace.

Decorations along the gracious entry hall create compelling focal points.

Visible from the entry hall, matching rosy-red sofas invite cozy fireside chats. Cheri Stith and Jamie Weyand created the mantel garland and other holiday décor.

Touches of red highlight the giant tree visible from the hall, living room, and dining room.

Treasures

Hanley Residence,
Scottsdale, Arizona
Mark Candelaria, architect

"Christmas décor should reflect your personal taste," says Nancy Hanley. "I select the Christmas décor for every room, and plan a style and look for each of the seven trees. All are artificial, but look entirely natural. The themes fall within a classic traditional look, using my favorite ornaments."

A tree in her grandchildren's playroom features a whimsical, red-and-white candy cane theme. This slender tree has festive candy cane garland woven throughout and is trimmed with treasured ornaments made over the years by Nancy's three children and seven grandchildren. The room's stuffed gingerbread dolls and elves add a playful touch.

The ten-foot Christmas tree in Nancy's living room is decorated with hundreds of tiny white lights. "It's brimming with shiny ornaments in various shades of gold, red, and burgundy. Exquisite ribbon intertwined throughout complements the ornaments. It is a pleasure to look at every day," she says.

Three classic pencil trees clustered in the library are surrounded with her grandchildren's teddy bears in many shapes and sizes. And in the breakfast room is an old-world-style country Christmas tree with tiny white lights in a large metal container. It contains Nancy's collection of multi-colored ornaments by MacKenzie-Childs, Christopher Radko, and Patricia Breen.

The Christmas tree in the upstairs game and television room is decorated with ornaments in soft shades of silver, beige, cinnamon, and blue, with dazzling silver ribbon that complements the colors in the room. Nancy says, "Although it is the least traditional of all of the trees in my home, it is beautiful to look at and makes the room feel very magical."

In some rooms, including on the dining room table and on windowsills, Nancy displays votive candles and groupings of slender, glittery tabletop trees in various heights and colors. Christmas trees may take center stage, but the staircase is elegantly decorated with garland of greenery, little white lights, and gorgeous ribbon. "It looks magnificent at night," says Nancy. "On the mantels, I like to use

garland that incorporates fresh magnolia leaves, or greenery with berries and little white lights."

One of her traditions is to hang personalized needlepoint Christmas stockings from the living room mantel for every family member, including the grandchildren. In addition to a gift in each stocking, a Christmas ornament is tied with ribbon to the outside of each stocking. "It's a great joy to celebrate the Christmas season with family and friends," she says.

A ten-foot-tall tree dominates the expansive Hanley living room. Custom needlepoint stockings for grandchildren hang at the mantel. *Photography by Julianne Palmer, Pearl Blossom Photography; courtesy Candelaria Design*

Nativity figures from Nancy's collection adorn tabletops.

Nancy placed three Christmas trees in the library. Their tiny white lights contrast elegantly with the dark wood walls. Bright red amaryllis adds a splash of color.

Nancy is fond of mini tabletop trees and displays groups of them on trays throughout her home. The centerpiece on the dining room table is a tray with a glittering assortment of trees. The footed tray on a refectory table beside a window wall displays nativity sculptures. Flanking the tray are collections of chunky candles on sculpture-like candlesticks.

Nancy's collection of Christopher Radko ornaments hangs on the breakfast room tree. The candle chandelier is crowned with greenery similar to that encircling a hurricane globe on the table. Candles and greenery add color to a cabinet top.

The newest tree in the Hanley home is the whimsically trimmed tree in the children's playroom. Toys galore keep it company.

Nancy trimmed the tree in the large second-floor game and television room in a contemporary style. It lends magic to the large family gathering space.

Fireplace mantels on patios are decorated with greenery. Wreaths accent some walls. A coffee table has a tray of candles and greenery; a hurricane lamp is surrounded by embellished greenery. The decorating does not interfere with spectacular views.

Cozy

Gawlik Residence,
Scottsdale, Arizona
Mark Candelaria, architect

"When decorating for the holidays, Bob and I just try to keep the style and feel of our home," says Mary Ellen Gawlik. It is traditional—sort of fancy, but not too fancy; pretty but comfortable. We choose the traditional warm, cozy colors of Christmas—red and green—plus gold that adds warmth and brightness to the tree and reflects the fabrics used in the living room."

The couple asked their architect Mark Candelaria, to make the back garden the focal point from the house. From the foyer, visitors can see a bank of French doors that open into a European-style garden with a fountain and pool. "When Christmas lights are added to the shrubs and flowers, the garden just glistens and radiates feelings of warmth and peace—truly a Christmas present," Mary Ellen says.

A see-through fireplace separates the living room and dining rooms, and mantels in each room are decorated, along with the dining room mirrors. "Our Christmas tree sits between these two rooms so that people can enjoy the glow of the lights from both angles," says Mary Ellen. "The tree is also visible from the veranda, through a wall of French doors. And lights on trees in the courtyard are visible indoors."

The dining and living room mantel decorations and twelve-foot St. Catherine woodland spruce and ornaments were purchased from Rustic Stuff. "The fun part is working with Paul Falk of Rustic Stuff. I decide what I want, and he and his people do the difficult work of hanging things all around," Mary Ellen says.

Architect Mark Candelaria designed the Gawlik house as a small Italian village nestled among embracing hills. Aglow for Christmas, the entrance with mirror-image stairs is spectacular and warmly inviting. *Photography by Julianne Palmer, Pearl Blossom Photography; courtesy Candelaria Design*

Traditional wreaths with bold red ribbons adorn the entry.

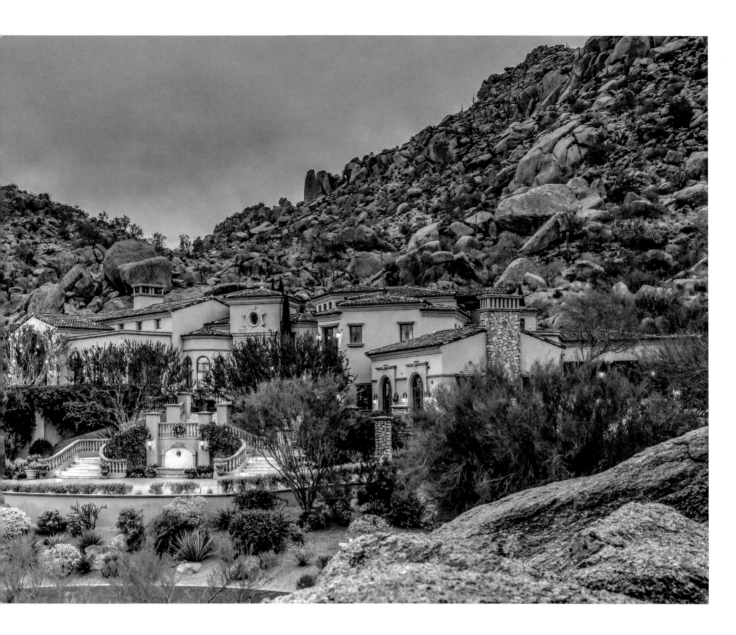

The massive St. Catherine spruce tree fills the living room with the fragrance of Christmas.

Robert and Mary Ellen take a moment for a keepsake photograph in front of the see-through fireplace, thoughtfully designed by their architect Mark Candelaria, top left.

At one end of the living room (and too large to be called merely a bar) is a fully equipped beverage center. A garland-festooned chandelier with charming red shades, a small table, and upholstered chairs create a cozy spot for a drink.

Show-stopping architectural features in the dining room include the dramatic arched ceiling and an oculus window with a deep reveal. Over the dining table hangs a spectacular crystal chandelier. A beautifully embellished garland frames the mirror over a sideboard.

Ribbon-trimmed greenery adorns the chandelier hanging from the herringbone brick ceiling in the extraordinary kitchen with black cabinets and twin islands.

In the breakfast area with mirrored ceiling, the chandelier's bold red ribbon echoes that of the Christmas tree in the adjoining family room.

Traditional Christmas colors prevail in the family room, The red ribbon tree topper echoes the red of the sofa and rug, enlivening the neutral color of stone and plaster walls.

A wreath graces a patio door, which overlooks the European-style garden. Decorated with colorful lights, the garden is enchanting at night.

Feliz

Gallagher Ranch,
San Antonio, Texas
Chris Hill, architect

Steeped in history, the 1800s Gallagher Ranch has served many purposes over the years—fortress, headquarters, working ranch, and dude ranch resort for movie stars. Its Christmas decorations are a nod to the days when Will Rogers, Orson Welles, Lily Pons of the Metropolitan Opera, and later, Prince Rainier and his wife Princess Grace were guests. In those early days, cedar beams in the living room were decorated with hanging moss. Today, simple garlands of seasonal greenery intertwined with fairy Christmas lights highlight the handsome, dark beams. "We migrated away from the traditional tree in favor of garlands with hand-blown glass ornaments from artisan Jake Zollie Harper of Zollie Glass Studio," says ranch owner and architect Chris Hill. Greenery and candles mingle with treasured objects on tabletops and cabinet shelves in the imposing room.

An avid collector, Chris created interiors that appear to have evolved over generations. A rich mix of art and artifacts gives the main house a distinctive, circa-nineteenth-century, south-of-the-border ambiance. "I have always felt that one of the best things about Texas is that it is close to Mexico," Chris says. "Certainly, a strong Mexican influence on this ranch is very natural. After all, ranch founder Peter Gallagher, who met Santa Ana in Galveston, was hired by Santa Ana to build a depot in San Antonio. I like to think that Santa Ana slept here," he says.

He was developing land in the Hill Country when someone urged him to look at this "cool place" a short drive from downtown San Antonio. Attracted by its "good vibes," he purchased the ranch and its three long-vacant buildings. Part of the ranch is under a conservation easement given to

Mexican-style structures give the ranch its south-of-the-border ambience. Downtown San Antonio is only a short drive away.
Exterior photographs by Barbara Justice

the Nature Conservancy in honor of his mother, Elizabeth Potter Hill. Over time, Chris has restored the buildings, with their twenty-five rooms. "It's been twenty years—time to start again," he says. In the meantime, Christmas Day calls for a celebratory meal.

The grand dining room is the setting for a Christmas dinner that includes handmade Coahuila-style tamales and champagne—along with a potluck of the traditional family dishes, including many Mexican favorites. "Always available during Christmas season are Marta's tamales, pork en salsa colorada, chicken in pepian verde, or refried bean and jalepeno," says Chris. It is Feliz Navidad at the Gallagher Ranch.

Walls of caliche (limestone), the ceiling of dark native timbers, and a Mexican Saltillo tile floor combine to create an interior that is both rustic and sophisticated. *Photograph by Natalia Sun*

Period sculpture and other art objects enhance the *casa grande* atmosphere in the large main room, part of the original 1800s hacienda. *Photograph by Natalia Sun*

A large blue-and-white Chinese porcelain ginger jar mixes elegantly with art and sculpture from Central and South America. *Photograph by Natalia Sun.*

The bold red of wide-open cabinet doors adds drama to the baronial dining room. Big pots of red geraniums brighten the table. *Photograph by Barbara Justice*

Royal poodles Pookie and Niki wait for Santa. *Photograph by Natalia Sun*

An eighteenth-century Italian chandelier and antique tapestry contribute to the grandeur of the dining room. In preparation for a festive meal, candles flicker amid centerpiece greenery and mantel garland. *Photograph by Natalia Sun*

Funfetti

Geyer Residence,
Frisco, Texas
Shay Geyer, interior designer

Christmas Eve is a busy time in the Geyer home. In the kitchen, Shay and her daughters, Jaylie and Brooklyn, are baking a special cake—a birthday cake for Jesus. "Jaylie and Brooklyn pick the cake and icing flavors," says Shay. "They usually choose a 'funfetti' cake—one with rainbow chip icing or strawberry with pink icing. They love to decorate it with lots of sprinkles. We leave Santa a slice of cake and a glass of milk." The wooden tree advent calendar is another family tradition. "My girls can't wait to open the door at the countdown each day to see what special prize waits within," she says. "It's usually small pieces of chocolate candies or little trinket toys."

An end table in the living room is the perfect spot for one of Shay's favorite decorations—a Christmas cloche with a nativity scene, given to her years ago by a friend. Shay has collected nutcrackers in various sizes and styles over the years. "I place them throughout our home according to color and size. Some have permanent homes because of their large size. Others move around, as

our younger daughter loves to play with them."

The fourteen-foot faux fir Christmas tree in the formal living room is topped with an angel in a gold gown. "I searched for years to find the perfectly scaled angel topper for our tall ceiling," Shay says. "My daughters both have horrible allergies, so we have to use faux trees. Both of my girls love to decorate the trees with me. They've learned all of my tricks

and techniques for tucking and placing ornaments just right.

Shay's technique involves grouping ornaments of various sizes, textures, and shapes together. She tucks the largest ornaments deep into the branches, then adds smaller sizes and more colors and textures. "I use ornament hangers to secure them and twist a piece of the branch around the top to help conceal the hanger," she says.

Each of Shay's daughters has a tree in their room. "They select the ornaments and other décor to coordinate with their bedroom decorating schemes. Jaylie loves the beach, turtles, and a casual look. Brooklyn loves dogs and anything with pink or sparkles."

Shay is partial to the tree and mantle décor in her master bedroom. "It's so peaceful to fall asleep in there with the garland and tree lights on," she says. "I love the rich but soft palette of blues accented with lavender."

The Geyers spend quite a bit of family time in the study,where a tall, slim fir was recently decorated with blue, malachite green, gold, and fuchsia to coordinate with the room.

Wrapping Christmas gifts is one of Shay's favorite activities. "It's actually a stress reliever for me. I go all out," she laughs. "I coordinate gift packaging with our trees. I mix solid color glitter papers with patterned papers. I have to hot glue the glitter paper seams when I wrap the presents. People think I'm crazy to do that, but it makes for the most beautiful packages. And it's a lot harder for the kiddos to sneak a peek at what is inside! My mom is a fabulous bow maker; I invite her over to help because her bows are always the best! We use wired ribbon so the bows hold their shape. We typically use solid color ribbon for patterned packages and patterned ribbon for solid papers, but we'll

mix it up, if it feels right." The beautifully gift-wrapped packages are an essential part of the Christmas tree scenario.

The Geyers typically exchange gifts to each other on Christmas Eve after the candlelight service at their church. Says Shay, "Our girls wake up Christmas morning to open gifts left them by Santa. We enjoy a formal Christmas day dinner with extended family and friends that evening." That dinner is a perfect highlight of a perfect season.

Lights on all the trees and shrubbery, around the roofline, across the balcony, and on the tree visible through the window illuminate Santa's path to the Geyer home. A stand-in sleigh awaits the real Santa. *Photography by Dan Piassick, courtesy IBB Design*

The colors in a contemporary painting above the period-style black hall chest inspired the holiday decor.

The living room's black wall is a strong counterpoint to ornaments in a plethora of vivid colors.

Shay limited this color palette to delightful cool blues and greens. Not all Christmas flowers are poinsettias!

Brian, Shay, Jaylie, Brooklyn (on her father's lap), and Roxy the boxer pose at the fireplace.

Gift wrapping is a favorite part of Christmas for Shay. Not all go under a tree. Some may highlight a coffee table—at least until gift-opening time.

Light on wreaths and the master bedroom Christmas tree cast a romantic glow. Shiny ornaments in exotic colors and metallic gold add sparkle and glamour.

Jaylie and Roxy await the moment those beautifully wrapped gifts can be opened. Jaylie's room is decorated with felt garland. The beaded topper on her tree is eye-catching, as are the stylized mini Christmas trees of dressmaker trim on her bathroom counter.

In Brooklyn's room, a nutcracker stands guard on the night stand.

In the breakfast room, midnight blue walls are a bold background for a mounted, white-beaded stag head with a bright red ribbon and a wreath of shiny gold ornaments. Hot pink ornaments and flowers stand out among a myriad of spirited colors.

Non-traditional cyclamen pink and cobalt blue ornaments compose the garland draped across a mantel. Saddle shaped stools hold colorful gift packages.

Lighted letters spell out the holiday mood at the Geyer home.

Tannenbaum

Galt Residence,
Brookhaven, Georgia
Melissa Galt, interior designer

Interior designer Melissa Galt typically designs one to three trees for a client's home, taking cues from the room décor and incorporating family heirloom ornaments. In her own home she decorates as many as six themed trees.

The Giving Tree in the great room is trimmed with white lights and hung with ornaments given to her at ornament parties.

The Spa Tree is done up in shades of green, blue, and silver ornaments with blue lights, and sits whimsically in the master bathtub. When the doors to the bath are left open, it offers a magical, twinkling focal point from the bedroom.

The Everything but the Kitchen Sink Tree is exactly that—a catch-all for family ornaments from years past and those picked up on travels around the world and locally. Wrapped in old-fashioned colored lights rather than LEDs, it brightens up the kitchen.

The Glass Tree, found in Indonesia, is made of glass fragments stacked and wired into a six-foot "tree" on a metal frame. An open cavity in the center fills with light when placed atop an up-light. This extraordinary tree weighs more than 200 pounds and is usually placed in the bedroom, where it casts a soft, luminous glow.

The Shimmer Tree is adorned exclusively with gold and silver ornaments and garlands of gold and silver snowflakes. Dressed in white lights, it sits on the landing at the top of the stairs above the foyer, providing a shimmering welcome to holiday guests.

Designer Melissa Galt (great-granddaughter of Frank Lloyd Wright) takes a break from Christmas decorating. *Photography by Robert Thien, courtesy Melissa Galt Interiors*

The Peacock Tree—with decorations in teals, purples, and greens (Melissa's favorite color combination)—livens up her office during the holidays, giving it a feeling of New Orleans at Mardi Gras.

Naturally, the first thing Melissa plans for is her trees. "First, I position each tree in its space, and then decorate the room around it with collections of nutcrackers, nativity scenes, assorted Santa Clauses, and garlands.

"My favorite ornaments are those made by my grandmother Catherine, who was Frank Lloyd Wright's daughter. Each is a one-of-a-kind diorama, and I put them in a huge basket. My grandmother, who has been gone for thirty-five years, also made two of the most divine angels ever of sheeting dipped in starch and then sprayed gold. I treasure those unique angels."

Melissa's trees evoke an array of moods. "The Giving Tree is nostalgic, with ornaments all provided by friends. The Shimmer Tree is elegant and dazzling; the glass tree is breathtaking. The

Everything but the Kitchen Sink and the Spa trees are decidedly fun," says Melissa. "My clients also mix styles and periods. Many have contemporary interiors, but still have a traditional tree with ornaments collected over the years."

Melissa recalls that during college, she had a live tree in her apartment. She went home for Christmas, leaving the tree up for two weeks without water, and returned to find a skeleton of a tree standing in the corner, with all the needles and ornaments on the floor. "Not one had broken! Imagine if I'd had a time lapse camera, it would have proved very entertaining to watch each one slowly roll off the tree and decorate the floor around it," she says.

The last year she had a real tree, she discovered that for at least a week, she'd been watering her favorite Tibetan rug and hardwood floor. "I heard a crash one night and raced downstairs to find my Giving Tree tipped over, bone dry. The watering gadget I was using had come out of the tree base. Fortunately, I only lost a couple of ornaments."

Melissa also decorates her living room mantel with tall, gold stylized trees, plus ball ornaments, lights, stockings, and more. "It's a scene stealer," she says. "The stair railing dressed in gold on evergreen and twinkling softly with holiday lights complements the mantel."

Christmas is everywhere in Melissa's living room. Even the reclining reindeer near the door wear Christmas necklaces.

The mantel boasts a Midas touch.

A nativity set and seasonal accessories are artfully arranged on shelves flanking the mantel.

Melissa's nutcracker collection marches up the stairs with a heavily garlanded railing. At the top of the stairs, next page, sits her "shimmering tree" trimmed in gold and silver ornaments.

A collection of prized ornaments and accessories adorn the table.

Melissa discovered her glass tree in Indonesia. A hollow in the bottom hides a light.

The spa tree takes up a whimsical position in the master bathtub.

Tradition

Labatt Residence,
San Antonio, Texas
Cheri Stith and Jamie Weyand, Christmas décor

Raven Labatt's husband grew up in their 1929 Tudor-style house, built for an army colonel stationed at Fort Sam Houston. "My husband's parents bought the house from him, and we bought it from my mother-in-law after my husband's father passed away seventeen years ago," says Raven, an interior designer. "We spent a year remodeling it. I love the fact that we have kept the house in the family. At Christmas, everyone can come back home."

Raven starts decorating for Christmas the week before Thanksgiving. "I have a team of talented elves, Cheri Stith and Jamie Weyand, who help decorate my mantels and the staircase," she

says. "They are true lifesavers! I fill in everywhere else with favorite items, including castle sculptures by local artist Nancy Pawell, which I've collected over many years. Every year, the day after Thanksgiving, my mom and I attend Nancy's show and I buy one or two castles."

An artificial tree is the best option because of family allergies, but evergreen clippings provide Christmas fragrance. "When I was first married, we had hardly any ornaments, so I used bows and balls all over the tree," she says. "Now, after twenty years of collecting Christopher Radko ornaments, I have a lot of them, many with a special meaning."

Raven says that as a designer, she comes across so many appealing objects that it's hard to stay with one look, so she mixes styles. In the eclectic entry, a red pagoda-shaped light fixture hints at the chinoiserie-influenced living room beyond. The holiday star of the living room, with its elegant Foo dogs and sculptural ginger jars, is a dramatic white tree trimmed with blue and white chinoiserie ornaments. A room adjoining the dining room is done in pinks and greens. "Our family room with eighteenth-century antiques and old world feel is decorated traditionally. But the white tree is whimsical—and fun!" she says.

Christmas lights flicker among the ivy that surrounds the entry of the Labatts' 1920s Tudor-style home. Decorative garlands and wreath embellish the recessed door.
Photography by Natalia Sun

The mantel's lavish white garland with interwoven blue ribbon emphasizes the blue-and-white theme of Raven's holiday décor.

Interior designer Raven Labatt's white Christmas tree is enhanced with blue-and-white ornaments inspired by her collection of blue-and-white Chinese porcelain.

Raven prominently displays her treasured
collection of castle sculptures by Nancy
Pawell.

The tree, garlands on the mantel, and a
collection of nutcrackers lend Christmas
spirit.

A lone star tops the traditional red-and-green decorated tree in the family room.

Stockings hang on both sides of the expansive fireplace—well away from flames.

Nutcrackers from the family's collection appear here, there, everywhere.

Tiny stylized Christmas trees add holiday
flair to the malachite powder room with
parrots and turtle faucet fittings.

Joy

Beach Residence,
Wichita, Kansas
Mitzi Beach, interior designer

Mitzi Beach has a vision—a room designed for Christmas with a natural theme. "It's pretty, calming, and inviting, with a less-is-more philosophy. It beckons my family and guests to come in and linger, enjoying my family heirlooms and special Christmas décor."

Bringing her vision to life means unboxing her collections and favorite decorations, making a list, and ordering live wreaths and poinsettias. Then, with everything at hand, "I am ready for the fun part—putting it all together."

Mitzi is "definitely a Christmas purist," so her color scheme is red and green. And the traditional sounds and scents of Christmas are important. "Adding music, candles, and wonderful kitchen and other aromas certainly layers on the reasons why we love Christmas decorating in our homes. Being an empty nester for many years now, I buy a small table-size live tree. I just have to relive that Christmas fragrance of real pine greenery."

Old favorite ornaments always adorn the tree, while new ornaments add interest or play up a theme. "Since I no longer have a large tree, I have blessed my adult children with their childhood ornaments," Mitzi says. "It is such a sweet thrill to see these ornaments in their homes now as part of their Christmas tradition."

The living room fireplace is a focal point. However, "my goal is to enhance my living room with the Christmas spirit, not to overpower the existing ambiance," she says. She returns to the principles of interior design. "Scale and proportion are essential in creating a lovely fireplace scene," she says. "This means large, medium, and small elements thoughtfully arranged. Seeing tons of items with no regard to proper design principles makes my teeth itch!"

"My main objective for all of my interior designing—and especially for Christmas—is to create a scene that portrays the true purpose of our homes, which is to make everyone feel welcome and comfortable," she says.

Designer Mitzi Beach, a "Christmas purist," sticks to a traditional red-and-green color scheme. *Photography by Shane Organ Photo, courtesy Mitzi Beach Interiors*

Mitzi orders her poinsettias from the florist well ahead of the holidays.

A bright red-berry wreath and "joy" plaque add Christmas cheer to the kitchen.

Red poinsettias on the buffet and red napkins on the table create a festive mood in the dining room. The centerpiece is a tableau of candles, greens, and small sculptures.

The entry to the Beach home is accentuated with columns wrapped in garland and topped with wreaths. Wreaths repeated on the porch railing above emphasize the entry and restate its welcome.

Classic

Lightfoot House at Colonial Williamsburg,
Williamsburg, Virginia

Christmas decorations at the Lightfoot House are a study in the colonial-era restrained elegance that makes Colonial Williamsburg a design mecca for designers. Garland swags hang in rhythmic scallops along the extraordinary Chippendale fence. The brick façade of the 1730s Georgian house is enlivened by wreaths on each of the eight twelve-over-twelve double-hung windows. Indoors, for a recent Spring Green Garden Club Christmas tour, simple bouquets of leaves and berries added touches of winter color now as they would have in the 1700s, when the winter season, rather than Christmas, was celebrated. The Christmas tree had not yet been discovered in the new world, so there is none in this house. One of the eighty-eight original buildings still standing, it was owned by three generations of the Lightfoot family. At one time it was the residence of the president of the Colonial Williamsburg Foundation, a center for hospitality that welcomed distinguished guests and government leaders from around the world.

The front door opens into a central passage. Flanking the passage and facing the street are a large parlor and dining room shown here. Furnishings throughout the house are from the Colonial Williamsburg collection and a reproduction program. Those who love the evergreen eighteenth-century style can shop online, via catalog, and at a shop in Colonial Williamsburg.

The circa 1730 Georgian-style Lightfoot House in Colonial Williamsburg would look at home today in any town in the United States. The Chinese-influenced Chippendale fence is noteworthy. *Photograph courtesy the Colonial Williamsburg Foundation*

The classic interiors of the Lightfoot house are a lesson in elegant restraint. Wreaths in the parlor window in colonial times would have been a nod to winter. In the central hall, a Chinese export porcelain bowl holds evergreens and berries that could have been found in colonial gardens. Holiday decorations were provided by Clark Taggart of the Colonial Williamsburg Floral Design Studio, and Don Haynie of Buffalo Springs Farm. *Photograph courtesy the Colonial Williamsburg Foundation*

Principal furnishings in the dining room and throughout the house are from the Colonial Williamsburg collection and reproduction program. *The Colonial Williamsburg Foundation*

Love

Stith Residence,
San Antonio, Texas
Cheri Stith, interior designer

Christmas season starts early for Cheri Stith, partner with Jamie Weyand in Feather, Fluff & Flings, which specializes in decorating for special occasions. The duo decorates dozens of homes in the Alamo City, starting in early November. She and her family begin decorating her own home the Friday after Thanksgiving. "Working nonstop, it usually takes four to five days to complete all the details," she says.

Cheri finds tradition comforting, so she changes only small things, such as ribbon combinations, from year to year. This year's "plaid tidings" theme played out in plaid and red velvet ribbons on the exterior, including the front door, and inside on the family room mantel. In the entry, a nativity scene is always displayed front and center.

While favorite ornaments and decorations appear every year, it's the newly acquired pieces that spark Cheri's creativity. Glass fruit objects of art found at a to-the-trade market in Dallas inspired the contemporary-looking mantel decorations in the master suite. "I decided to mix them with wonderful balls in some of the same colors in the Manuel Canavos fabrics in our bedroom," she says. "The colors are extraordinary and they make me so happy!"

A tree in the sitting room showcases Christopher Radko and glass ornaments, along with needlepoint ornaments Cheri has made over the years. The tree topper is a show stopper: the crown and scepter from her days as a duchess in Buccaneer Days in Corpus Christi. After Cheri's daughter was also in Buccaneer Days several years ago, her train was repurposed as the tree skirt for the white-flocked tree in the sunroom, which is topped with her crown. The tree, a gift from Cheri's college roommate, contains colorful vintage glass ornaments collected at estate sales or at Round Top, the famous annual Texas flea market.

Cheri and her family host a party during the holiday season each year. Her favorite celebration was in 2017, which coincided with her husband's sixtieth birthday. "A visit from Santa and Mrs. Claus surprised everyone, including my husband," she says. "Mrs. Claus read *The Night Before Christmas* to our guests. Santa read the Christmas story from the Bible. He then spoke about how Christ came to bring light into the world, and encouraged everyone to go out into the world and shine their lights. From his velvet pack, we passed out red-and-green glow necklaces to all the guests, who put them on. That brought me great joy."

At designer Cheri Stith's home, outsized exterior decorations boldly proclaim the season. *Photography by Natalia Sun*

The sitting room tree displays Cheri's cherished collection of Christopher Radko ornaments. The tree topper is the crown she wore as a Corpus Christi Buccaneer Days duchess.

Crystal glassware adds sparkle to the coffee table.

Instead of flowers as a centerpiece, Cheri surrounds a collection of stylized white Christmas-tree cones with greenery and interesting objects and ornaments.

The family room fireplace shares the spotlight with a garlanded cabinet and pots of bright red poinsettias.

Nutcrackers steal the show in [ ] room.

The white sunroom tree displays Cheri's collection of vintage glass ornaments. On a shelf are favorite sculptures.

Ornaments in the mantel garland repeat the colors found in the richly patterned drapery.

Retro

Plantation Residence,
Adel, Georgia
Dustin Van Fleet, interior designer

"I love lived-in spaces that everyone, young and old, can enjoy," says Dustin Van Fleet, interior designer and owner of FUNK Living, a retail shop. "I always pitch an elegant yet country-casual approach to holiday decorating—traditional style with a whimsical twist. I've built my design style and career on sophisticated fun, whimsy, and nostalgia—generally thought of as retro or vintage. I can't even imagine a contemporary Christmas in my house."

He often plans a theme for clients based on what's readily available in their natural surroundings. "The majority of my decorating time is spent wandering around vast grounds finding and gathering the perfect natural elements," he says. And he's been collecting handmade decorations in natural materials for the better part of two decades. "My tradition is to add at least six different natural elements to my existing collection each year," he says.

Rather than making the tree the centerpiece, he focuses his attention on "snow"-dusted arrangements that combine fruit, cotton, and live garden cuttings—apples, pears, magnolia, dogwood, cedar, and other greenery. Live magnolia or boxwood garlands are often draped across the mantel and onto the floor on either side, and swags spill out of chandeliers. Garlands are stuffed with fresh fruit, pinecones, and cranberries.

"Get me a magnolia wreath and red-and-white polka-dot ribbon for a bow, and I'm in Christmas decorating heaven. You know, it's the simple things in life!" he says.

Designer Dustin Van Fleet, owner of the retail shop FUNK Living, specializing in vintage furnishings and fashions. *Photography by Watson Brown, courtesy Dustin Van Fleet/FUNK Living*

Dustin's mission in decorating a plantation home owned for generations by the same family was to refresh, not change, vintage interiors. Of the more-is-better school of design, he added more! The dining room mantel was treated to a swath of wide ribbon, a bouquet of roses, and oranges. Behind the fireplace fender are pots of poinsettias. A flower-filled large silver urn on a silver platter adds drama to the dining table.

The picturesque entry sports a Dustin-designed wreath outside and in.

A bouquet in the entry hall includes what looks like stalks of cotton with open bolls!

A lavish garland of native greenery embellished with a variety of flowers adorns the living room mantel.

A wreath graces the red side door.

Victorian

Vollmer Residence,
Brentwood, Tennessee
Howard Wiggins, Christmas décor

"Howard knows just what to do to enhance a space," says Jenny Vollmer, owner of Jenny Vollmer by Design, a popular Nashville event planner. She hired Howard Wiggins of Howard Wiggins Interiors in Brentwood, Tennessee, to update and decorate her Victorian-style interior for an annual open-house fundraising event. Known as a master of color, Howard began by painting the tea room ceiling a coral color. "I was a little startled. That had never occurred to me, but I love it," says Jenny.

Above some framed nineteenth-century stump work, Howard placed an ornate gold cherub sculpture crowned with lavish garland. Fresh fruit adds drama to the fireplace mantel, and a garland surrounds the front door, obscuring the sidelights. "It's very pretty and welcoming, and since people can't see inside, there's a heightened sense of expectation," says Jenny, who opens her Brentwood home to the Literacy Council of Williamson County and to Global Rise, a nonprofit that feeds hungry children through agricultural initiatives. Once visitors step inside, the decorated grand staircase and entryway make a stunning first impression.

Jenny places a Christmas tree in every room. "I probably would do that even if there were no tours!" says Jenny.

For his part, Howard has been inspired by visits to the Queen Anne Victorian-style Heritage House in Riverside, California, and the Biltmore estate in Asheville, North Carolina. "I definitely prefer faux trees and recommend them to busy clients like Jenny," he says. "Faux trees need no maintenance and stay fresh-looking throughout the long, active holiday season."

Jenny and designer Howard Wiggins await open-house guests.

Event designer Jenny Vollmer opens her home each Christmas for a fundraising tour. *Photography by Reid Rolls, courtesy Howard Wiggins Interior Design*

Designer Howard Wiggins created the tier displaying sweet treats in the entry hall. Faux white poinsettias accent a garland on the stair railing.

For Jenny's tea room, her favorite for entertaining friends, Howard trimmed two trees. Both are in Victorian style—one with tea cups, the second tree ropes of pearls.

There is always at least one tree in every room, no two trimmed alike. The tree in the red living room is trimmed in traditional red and green.

Neo-Classical

Stone Residence,
San Antonio, Texas
Leland Stone, designer

The storied Roosevelt Library lends its own considerable charm to the most magical time of the year. Once the second branch library of San Antonio, the Roosevelt Library is now the private residence of Leland Stone and his partner, Neil Schneuker. After Leland purchased the property in 2013, he restored and repurposed the Spanish colonial revival library as a residence and exhibit space for architectural finds. In 2016, he formed the Roosevelt Library Social Club, solidifying the library's role as a favorite San Antonio social gathering spot.

The Christmas décor honors the 300 French neo-classical plaster ornaments that hang from the branches of the Christmas tree. "These unique decorations, typically used to adorn walls and ceilings, are plaster impressions of wood molds made by European artisans in the late nineteenth century by Decorators Supply, a Chicago firm still in existence," says Leland, principal of Stone Standard, a firm specializing in fine architectural hardware and plumbing fittings. "I had the

pieces recast especially for Roosevelt Library as Christmas tree ornaments. All we needed to do was apply the ribbon."

Clusters of berries and sprigs enliven tree branches, redolent of an earlier age when decoration was simple and natural. Preserved fondant flowers from Leland's mother's wedding cake are placed near the top. At the tree's base is a kaleidoscope pouf crafted of fine European fabrics from KBK To-The-Trade. It's a fitting background for the display of handcrafted miniature buildings and figurines comprising a rural Japanese village, Leland's elegant version of the Victorian-era German *putz* village (from the German *putzen*, meaning "to decorate"). Leland's father was a hospital administrator in Tokyo, where Leland was born, and where Leland's mother acquired the exquisite pieces. The toy bear at the tree base belonged to Leland's father.

Leland follows in the footsteps of his great-great-grandfather, who started a hardware business in San Antonio in the 1850s. In the

spacious grand hall, where the principal dining area is located, a custom French gallery system displays the firm's legacy hardware from around the world. The Roosevelt Library's full-time staff—a butler, two under-butlers, and a chef who loves his recently installed Chateau 180 La Cornue stove—are on hand for nightly formal dinners. For these elegant affairs, Leland commissioned one hundred place settings of silver-plate cutlery based on pieces from his grandmother's sterling silver set. When the weather turns icy, as it can in San Antonio, a roaring fire warms the library, and intimate dinners are held in front of the fireplace.

"Roosevelt Library is busy year-round," says Leland, "but never more so than during the enchanted holiday season, when the library is the perfect setting for festive gatherings."

A grand tree on a custom silk pouf takes pride of place in the main room of the historic Roosevelt Library, now the private residence of Leland Stone. *Photography by Natalia Sun*

156   STONE RESIDENCE

The main room—both showroom and dining room—is the scene of dinners prepared by Leland's chef. A mass of votive candles is an elegantly simple and romantic holiday centerpiece.

Custom ornaments decorate the tree. Near the top is a bouquet of fondant flowers preserved from the wedding cake of Leland's mother.

A miniature Japanese village, a memento of Leland's birth and early life in Tokyo, sits at the base of the tree.

Leland, right, and partner Neil Schneuker enjoy dinner before the fireplace. The silver service belonged to Leland's mother.

Green

Storey Residence,
Marks, Mississippi
Marilyn Trainor Storey, interior designer

"Green has always been one of my most favorite colors. It signifies life, healing, and rebirth—a perfect symbol of Christmas and our fertile delta area," says interior and textile designer Marilyn Trainor Storey. Its symbolism has been especially meaningful since a harrowing holiday experience in 2015.

As she recalls, "On the afternoon of December 23, I was putting the finishing touches on everything. I was listening to Christmas music, wrapping a few last-minute gifts, and baking. I was decanting a brand-new bottle of Crème de Menthe, a longtime Christmas tradition (and a key to my green color scheme). I had layered my Christmas dinner table with heirloom linens, china, crystal, and fresh flowers. To that gloriously decorated table, I added the last detail—red bird ornament favors, a favorite of my paternal grandmother who believed red birds to be spirits of ancestors watching over us. I was enjoying every little detail. Within thirty minutes, it was all swept away by a mighty wedge tornado."

Not only were the table and great room destroyed, the rest of the house did not fare well, either. "Thankfully, bracing literally at the last second in an interior bathroom, we were unharmed. Needless to say, we were especially thankful that Christmas," she says.

Two years later, spending Christmas in her Clarksdale studio and apartment while her country home was being reconstructed, she chose a color scheme of greens with gold, silver, gray, black, and white accents, echoing the design scheme for her home-in-progress. Green really pops when paired with elemental neutral and metallic colors, she says.

Marilyn experimented with green-toned pillow and table linen fabrics from her new textile line, including Grassy Fields (Coldwater Collection), French Garden (Grayton Collection), and Envious Rose (Floradora collection). Neutral-colored Pearl Girl (Grayton Collection) and Faux Bois (Coldwater Collection) fabrics accented the greens. Gilded

Designer Marilyn Trainor Storey

Shell from her Gilded Collection amped up the décor and added a modern edge and a Christmas feel. Throughout, liberal doses of decorative objects and architectural antiques served as a backdrop for Christmas glass ornaments on glittery, gold trees.

Marilyn set her Christmas dinner table with vintage china, antique oyster plates, and antique linens. "Small commissioned paintings of angels were favors," she says. "The angels have indeed watched over us! Fresh flowers, greens, and fruits, in keeping with my green color scheme, were the natural finishing touch. And yes, Ed and I (the Pearl Girl) devoured our traditional dozens of oysters before dinner, enjoyed a classic homemade grasshopper pie for dessert, and passed the Crème de Menthe as our postprandial. Our house, with its new green roof and green front door, would soon welcome us back home. We are always thankful. It is a Green Christmas!"

The gold art above the antique hall tree is by Delta artist Randall Andrews. The snake art is by Dwight Peacock, another Delta artist. Handmade stockings hang from the hall tree. Walking sticks are family heirlooms.
Photography courtesy MS Design Maven

The stone-top entry hall table is a rescued antique. On the tray are original sculptural busts. The black-and-white hardware cabinet is vintage with its original finish.

In the living room lounge, massive antique Mississippi pocket doors saved by Marilyn's father from the trash are hinged as a screen. Vintage prints of Venus hang on the screen. Velvet pillows on custom silver sofas are made of Marilyn's Golden Buckle fabrics.

A vintage wing chair with new green feet is covered in Marilyn's Grassy Fields fabric, which has a stylized cotton boll motif. Pillows are covered in her French Garden and Queen Bee fabrics.

A table remade with antique Venetian legs discovered in New Orleans is set for Christmas Eve supper a deux. Chairs upholstered in emerald green belonged to Marilyn's father.

The dining room dessert server is laden with small treasures, including vintage and antique china and silver and antique architectural fragments. Tiny white marble compotes hold vintage green ornaments. Glass containers hold paper-white bulbs.

The dining table is a glorious mix of vintage and mid-century china, family heirloom silver flatware, Waterford crystal and silver goblets, and Depression-era emerald-green Burple glasses. Napkins are monogrammed in Marilyn's favorite green. Flower arrangements include rosemary for remembrance.

Marilyn's famous grasshopper pie.

Marilyn's Easy Grasshopper Pie

Crust:
1½ cups + 1 tablespoon chocolate wafer crumbs, divided
5 tablespoons butter, melted

Combine 1½ cups of the wafer crumbs with the melted butter. Press into an ungreased 9-inch pie pan. Bake at 350 degrees for 5 to 7 minutes. Cool.

(I confess sometimes I just buy a chocolate cookie crumb crust if I'm in a big hurry.)

Filling:
2 cups marshmallow cream
2 cups heavy whipping cream
2 tablespoons clear Crème de Cacao
¼ cup green Crème de Menthe

In a large mixing bowl, whisk together the marshmallow cream, Crème de Menthe, and Crème de Cacao until smooth. In a separate bowl, whip cream until soft peaks form. Fold the whipped cream into the marshmallow mixture. Pour the combined mixture into the cooled chocolate crust. Decorate the top of the pie with the reserved cookie crumbs.

Freeze at least two hours until firm, or ideally overnight. Remove from the freezer 20 minutes before serving to thaw slightly. Garnish with fresh mint leaves and Andes chocolate mint candies for an extra festive Christmas touch. And, of course, serve with a cordial glass of Crème de Menthe.

The green velvet camelback sofa in the library belonged to Marilyn's father. Above it hangs a painting of Romulus and Remus of Roman mythology. On the ottoman/coffee table are favorite books. A forked crape myrtle branch hangs on a side wall.

A preserved boxwood wreath is suspended by 1970s millinery ribbon in front of a vintage white mirror. The console below is from the Duke Estate in North Carolina. A vintage Northern European metal basket contains an oystershell ball.

Marilyn uses the twelve-foot-long green table (an antique from a Mississippi Delta cotton gin) for serving. The portrait of Marilyn above the table was painted by Christopher Keywood. Decanters on a silver tray hold Christmas spirits, including an emerald-green vintage Italian Empoli.

Natural

Eddington Residence,
Little Rock, Arkansas
Rhonda Peterson, interior designer

Rhonda Peterson's clients, Ramsey and Ruth Eddington, live in a house perched on a hillside with views of the woods, the Arkansas River, and Pinnacle Mountain. "Though they are traditionalists, they appreciate shiny finishes, metallics, clean lines, and tighter, structured silhouettes," Rhonda says. She created a winter wonderland with twig "trees," pine cones, a gold and snow-frosted reindeer, and snow. The clients trimmed their tree with textural burlap poinsettias, gold berryleaf branches, bronzed glitter, and gold ornaments.

"There is something to be said for keeping the color theme monochromatic, like my client's home," Rhonda says. "In a monochromatic setting, the Christmas tree can be trimmed in any color. But since the important thing about color is to be true to oneself, if a client is a Skittles enthusiast (every color in the rainbow), I work with that.

In her own home, Rhonda decorates two trees. The tree in the living room is contemporary, trimmed with an "of the moment" color scheme and ornaments. The tree in the family room is traditional, with a red-and-green color scheme and a mix of favorite ornaments. The mantel is always the star. "Whether a mantel is dressed to the nines or simple, it should be dressed," says Rhonda. "Where there is no mantel as focal point, I create one. A console table is an excellent stand-in for a mantel. What matters most is decorating it to capture attention, hold interest, and create a moment for pause."

Rhonda encourages clients to mix old with new decorations. "It's very nostalgic to include old favorites—not just favorite ornaments for the tree, but beloved decorations throughout the house. Mixing in new ornaments brings a fresh, interesting look and mood that gives older ornaments renewed appeal."

Evergreen wreaths embellished with a single white faux poinsettia welcome guests to the Eddington home at Christmas. *Photography by Reggie Hameth*

A large wreath on the wall and pinecones hung by ribbon from a sconce decorate the entry hall.

Interior designer Rhonda Peterson creates a mini-forest tableau with reindeer sculpture on a console.

The living room tree is trimmed in tactile burlap poinsettias. Gold ornaments add shine.

Small touches of red in gift wrap trim and a vase of roses add a touch of color to the neutral scheme.

Rhonda checks decorations in the dining room, where a simple garland frames the window. Seasonal greens are the base for the pinecone centerpiece.

The stylish gray kitchen, decorated simply with a wreath at the window.

A vase of red flowers and berries and a sprig of greenery on plates bring cheer to the breakfast room table.

A green wreath above the bed adds a gentle holiday note to the serene master bedroom.

A red poinsettia and garland along the railing enlivens the porch, with its treasured view of the river and hills.

Nostalgic

Little Cottage,
San Antonio, Texas
Tim Little, interior designer

Designer Tim Little and Alex Perez, his business partner at TX Luxury Interiors, are typically booked solid decorating clients' homes for the holidays—once working on Christmas Eve to finish. That means he has to put up his own decorations in September, which he says helps him gear up to do his best work for clients.

The extended season also means he uses artificial trees in his home. Tim has been collecting vintage ornaments for decades and decorates with Shiny Brite ornaments from the 1950s, '60s, and '70s, as well as beaded snowflakes and mercury glass. Beneath the tree in Tim's living room sits a Raggedy Andy doll, which he received as a Christmas present in the early 1970s. "Destined to be my companion and friend for many Christmases to come, he sits at the base of my tree to remind me of my past and to be filled with love and hope," he says.

The house's name, Little Cottage, is a reference to Tim's name, but it also speaks to the quaint charm of the Tudor revival style, built around a home-and-hearth concept, he says. Constructed in 1929, the original layout is still intact. "The grand arches, charming fireplace, and intimate spaces are all about traditional family gatherings," he says. "I decorate with a reference to the past, but always strive to push the envelope further, with no rules except to love the process, love the materials I'm working with, and to err on the side of excess!"

Because his design work keeps him busy throughout December, Tim celebrates Christmas in January. "I usually have a Christmas party in mid-January. This allows more of the people I love to attend, and it gives me time to truly pour out the best hospitality I can offer," he says. "I celebrate with family and dear friends. The date is not important, since we gather to celebrate the love that binds us all together."

After decorating dozens of clients' homes for Christmas, designer Tim Little pauses to toast the season. *Photography courtesy TX Luxury Interiors*

Arched openings, cozy rooms, and a charming fireplace are a few of the things that Tim loves about his 1929 home.

Tim's tree is decorated with a favorite collection of Shiny Brite ornaments. The Raggedy Andy doll was a gift in the 1970s.

Tim loves decorating with ribbon, which can be reused from year to year. He uses it profusely for garland.

Designer touches in the dining room include fairy lights on the ficus tree, berry-laden branches tucked into chandelier arms, and a multi-element centerpiece displayed on a footed silver tray. The secretary near the table gets it own decorations.

Gilded

Atlanta Homes & Lifestyles Show House,
Atlanta, Georgia
Patricia McLean, interior designer

Patricia McLean describes her style as "old school," and it's evident in the master suite she designed for *Atlanta Homes & Lifestyles* magazine's Home for the Holidays show house. It features a rich antique Serapi rug in peach, terra-cotta, soft blues, and gold, which set the palette for the room. Farrow and Ball's Shaded White paint for walls was the perfect foil for the luscious colors used to decorate the spaces.

In front of the triple window at the front of the room is an antique gondola-style bench hand-carved in walnut. "It's laden with four embellished velvet pillows. One Fortuny pillow adds a pop of color. Colefax and Fowler draperies in blue linen with rich cream and gold silk velvet overlays hang from gold drapery rods with fleur de lis finials— uber lush framing for the vignette. A natural-greens wreath with a big gold bow is the finishing touch."

A fabulous bed is the natural focal point of any master bedroom. This sumptuous example is flanked by antique Coromandel screens. She chose Italian embroidered sheets and an elegant silk cover that evoke images of a good winter's nap. Patricia collects Christmas books. "The Metropolitan Museum Angel Tree is one of my favorite things to see at Christmas. I placed a picture book of the history of the Metropolitan Museum's Angel Tree by the bedside, and enjoyed telling visitors about it. It is one of the most inspirational Christmas scenes ever."

Across from the bed is an antique Provencal chest in a light cream color with a faux marble top in terra-cotta tones. Nearby is the room's main attraction—the eight-foot-tall, seven-foot-wide Fraser fir Christmas tree. "The chest perfectly compliments the big, green tree," says Patricia. "The tree is heavily decorated, which is how I like it."

It features old-fashioned metallic balls in silver, gold, and bronze, with some light-blue balls in the colors of the rug, sparkly crystal balls, and several hundred white lights. The "star" at the top was inspired by the Venetian starburst mirror above the chest. Presents are wrapped in gold and light-blue paper with blue satin and metallic gold bows.

"I love the idea of naps in the master bedroom with the glow of only Christmas lights," Patricia says. "To me, the tree is the most important part of decorating for Christmas. I am happy to know that this one brought joy to so many, including the children at Children's Healthcare of Atlanta, which the show house benefited."

Designer Patricia McLean displayed a favorite book from her collection in her Show House master suite. *Photography by Mia McCorkle, courtesy Patricia McLean Interiors, Inc.*

An antique Serapi rug set the palette for the bedroom.

The giant tree fills one corner of the room.

A Frazier fir wreath hangs above the antique gondola-style bench in the bedroom.

The romantic French-style dresser and stunning antique mirror create a memorable vignette.

A Fraser fir wreath hangs from a chain in the master bath's triple window. Silver ribbon accents the polished nickel fixtures. A metal Christmas tree with colored stones as ornaments stands guard at the lady's sink.

Tropical

Contemporary Residence,
West Palm Beach, Florida
Keith Carrington, interior designer

"A well-thought-out plan is a necessity in my book—of course straying from it is where magic can occur," says Keith Carrington. "Traditional does not have to be boring, Christmas décor should be as much fun as one can get away with." The fun starts with what Keith calls his "skittelicious" approach to color. "All colors are welcome in my life. Embrace all color combinations. Let your imagination run wild. Explore colors you may not typically use."

A designer with a penchant for the whimsical, Keith says: "If I had a chimney in Florida, I would get a pair of long black boots and dangle them inside the fireplace, revealing a hint of a bright red coat with white mink trim. The mantel should be decorated with gusto—garlands, swags, and whimsy." Alas, there's no fireplace, but Keith compensates with a larger-than-life Christmas tree.

Keith prefers real trees and says that old-fashioned flocking helps hold the needles in place, though finding a florist to do that may present a challenge these days.

When it comes to decorating his tree, Keith might revisit an old favorite theme, but change it up with new, colorful ornaments or ribbon. "Repurposing is the way to go if you are on a budget," he says. "Look at each object in a new way, its placement on the tree, and edit as you go."

Keith does not decorate his stairs, preferring to let them reflect his year-round style. However, he says, "If you're drawn to decorating your stairs, swag it up; just be careful your ball gown doesn't get caught up on the descent!"

Interior designer Keith Carrington mixes seasonal red and Palm Beach pastels with aplomb. *Photography by Nicholas Sargent, courtesy Keith Carrington Interiors*

Texture is important in Keith's holiday mantel design, which contrasts vibrant native greens and soft pastels.

Gold adds shimmer to a mirrored tabletop.

Keith includes the pool cabana in his holiday decorating scheme, then takes time for a refreshing dip.

A lavish collection of decorative holiday
accessories (including Keith's favorite
reindeer) makes the skirted round table a
dramatic focal point.

The absence of a fireplace is not a problem
for Keith, who hangs his stocking from an
antique mirror. A bowl of favorite Christmas
ornaments adds color.

Keith's lavish table setting and a
breathtaking sunset view makes Christmas
dinner a romantic, unforgettable event.

Fairyland

Tips Residence,
San Antonio, Texas
Kristin Tips, Christmas décor

Spreading holiday cheer is something of a mission for Kristin and Dick Tips. Their Terrell Hills residence on a prominent corner of the neighborhood is a holiday dream come true. Exterior walls are swathed in a rhythmic array of garlands and wreaths. Seasonal greenery adorns the grounds. The glorious grouping of poinsettias at the corner offers a perfect winter wonderland backdrop for family photos and selfies by those who make a special trip to see this home. At night, brilliant Christmas lights highlight the exterior décor. Trees wrapped in colorful lights—red, green, white, blue—are a beacon that transforms fellow citizens into tourists eager to see this magical fairyland!

Tall nutcrackers and tree-shaped decorations flank the custom glass entry door. The exterior of this grand house retains its vintage style, but the interior is a tribute to the couple's creativity. Dick, CEO of Mission Park Funeral Chapels and Cemeteries, has a passion for architecture (his grandfather was an architect). Kristen overseas the Tips family's Fairmont Hotel. The couple gutted, re-designed, and renovated the house, located on the street where he grew up, to accommodate the couple's twin children and provide an elegant event space.

Visitors step into a two-story demilune foyer that opens onto a mirrored hallway running the length of the home. Holiday cheer can be found in nearly every nook and cranny. Greenery and garlands, fresh floral bouquets, and bountifully decorated Christmas trees enliven the public spaces. Private spaces—the master suite sitting area, guest rooms, and the children's bedrooms and playroom—are also treated to Christmas decorations.

While the couple are known for their parties, it is their family moments that make the holiday special. "Kristin and I make it a point to spend time with our children and read the Bible to them before bed," Dick says. "We emphasize the spiritual meaning of Christmas."

Dick and Kristin Tips's Terrill Hills home is a well-known landmark at Christmas.
Photography by Natalia Sun

Ornaments on the white Christmas tree echo the dynamic blue color scheme of the Great Room seating area.

A luxurious garland and needlepoint stockings grace the fireplace in the red living room.

A hand-blown Murano glass chandelier, purchased on a trip to Murano, Italy, stars in the round dining room.

Ormolu ornaments decorate the counter separating the kitchen from the seating area in the great room.

The wrought iron light fixture above the kitchen island is hung with faux flora.

The children's tree has a special place in the breakfast area.

Dining room French doors open to an intimate courtyard decorated with pots of white poinsettias.

A sumptuous bow of Schiaparelli pink ribbon tops the tree in the daughter's bedroom.

In the son's room, a favorite toy keeps the Christmas tree company.

Christmas décor in the master bedroom sitting
area underscores the room's muted colors.

Country

Stonesthrow,
St. Louis, Missouri
Robert Basich, Christmas décor

Stonesthrow, the 120-acre farm of Bob and Liz Baisch, seems a world away from their Baisch and Skinner wholesale flower business headquarters in St. Louis, yet it's just a thirty-minute drive. The setting is idyllic—a valley surrounded by a state park and a state wildlife reservation encompassing more than 3,000 acres. A hundred-year-old bridge is the only way in and out of the valley, giving their farm an isolated, Shangri-la feeling. Natural cedar roping from the great Northwest and natural swags and lanterns decorate the bridge for the holidays. When the pond freezes over, neighbors gather to skate. Then an old cast-iron caldron is fired up and the gazebo (trimmed simply in pine) becomes a warming place. "Wreaths are hung from our outhouse and entrance gates as well as the carriage house. The focal point of outdoor decorations is a red German sleigh. It's been used at various venues throughout St. Louis," says Bob, who is also a talented floral designer.

Christmas Stonesthrow style is traditional red-and-green, country casual, and genuinely nostalgic. In the foyer, the stair banister is draped with fresh magnolia garland. The window treatment here and throughout the house consists of fresh, double-faced boxwood wreaths from North Carolina. "I feel strongly about keeping things simple and fresh," says Bob. "Too much and you lose sight of the details. I get overwhelmed with too much stuff."

There is one Christmas tree—live, of course. Located in the family room, it is trimmed with a variety of family ornaments.

"They're old favorites—most have a family memory tied to them," says Liz. The fireplace, home to all eleven grandchildren's stockings, is draped with fresh bay leaf garland. The setting contains a small collection of polo mallets family members have used over the decades.

In keeping with Bob's love of simplicity, the large fireplace in the Great Room is draped with fresh Christmas greens and berries and flanked by two black lanterns, which are lit during Christmas celebrations.

The cast-iron chandelier over the dining room table is a favorite item to decorate. "With eleven grandchildren, we have begun hanging fairy ornaments from the chandelier," says Liz.

"In addition to greens throughout the room, we add antlers found on the property, an assortment of cones, berries from Wisconsin, and pheasant feathers collected each year from pheasant hunting trips to South Dakota," Bob adds. The wine room doors, made from a variety of salvaged materials, are draped with hops.

During the holidays the whole house is magical, but one room is special. "The bar is our favorite gathering spot," says Bob. "Guests are greeted by our stuffed ferret, Estelle, given to us by a family friend. She adds a bit of glamour with her diamond choker and attitude-with-cigarette." Around the bar hangs mounted wildlife culled from the property, while cast-iron Foxy Fran watches over the pours with a smile.

Christmas decorations brighten the private approach to Stonesthrow, the Baisch country house. The bridge is the only way into the farm. The antique red German sleigh and gazebo are focal points. *Photography by Brian Farmer*

Seasonal greenery is a favorite decorating element for Bob Baisch, owner of a large wholesale florist business.

Red flowers decorate the hall chandelier and a wall shelf.

A truly great room welcomes family and friends to Christmas at Stonesthrow.

Fairy ornaments hang from the lavishly decorated iron chandelier over the dinner table with its view through double doors of the woods beyond.

Bob Baisch says the bar is a favorite hangout during the holidays. A collection of hand-painted plates surround the outside of the door into the bar. On the interior a garland of greenery adds holiday fragrance.

Stockings hang from the mantel in the sitting area.

In the television room, more stockings decorate the fireplace.

Horses are important to weekends and holidays at the farm. Near the Christmas tree is a collection of polo mallets.

There may be more greenery than blossoms at Christmastime, but the flowers steal the show.

Collectible

Parker and d'Andrimont Residence,
Lakewood, Colorado
Johanna Parker, Christmas décor

"The look I create has to be playful," says Johanna Parker, artist and designer of collectible ceramic sculptures that make delightful decorative accessories. "My characters work with a range of styles and suit a variety of personalities. In each, a pinch of whimsy blends humor and nostalgia to capture the hearts of holiday decorators eager to add magic and sweetness to their homes."

At the home Parker shares with her husband and business partner, J. P. d'Andrimont, her penchant for art décor and art nouveau pulls her toward vintage-style decorating. Old mercury glass baubles, bottle brush trees, vintage retro figurines, and other timeworn novelties are part of the merry mix.

Fearless when it comes to color, Johanna says. "My color palette dances around the traditional red and green themes. I enjoy adding shades and highlights of these hues, but for a touch of sparkle I mix in silvers and other metallics. For extra shimmer, I often use creamy white mica to accent the main palette and conjure more winter magic. At holiday time, we are celebrating the light, so I add glowing candles and twinkling Christmas lights for extra warmth and comfort."

The mantel is an ideal spot for showcasing her collection of holiday folk art characters. She mixes texture and a sense of the past with favorite pottery finds. Vessels are filled with branches hung with baubles and ornaments, which add movement and interest.

Johanna decorates windowsills with evergreen tips snipped from bushes and trees in her yard. "I create a nest on each windowsill and in it place seasonal objects—ruby pomegranates or red apples."

With a tiny cottage and a curious cat, she says, the choice of an artificial Christmas tree is a no-brainer, especially now that she has inherited her mother's childhood tree—"a white 1950s faux delight that I had decorated since I was a little girl. Today, it's our beloved tree that I load with a blend of my old and new folk art ornaments and vintage baubles." Some of her favorites include vintage mercury glass baubles and holiday characters—both finds and family hand-me-downs. To connect with nature, Johanna and J. P. often decorate a live evergreen tree in their yard with red baubles that dance in the wind. "It's a delight for the neighbors, and we can watch the tree grow, year after year," she says.

Collectibles designer Johanna Parker lives surrounded by her creations. In the living room, vintage baubles and beads hang from the 1930s chandelier. By the fire are 1930s chairs covered in red mohair and a vintage rocker that belonged to Johanna's grandmother. Santa and snowman mugs are from her Transpac Imports 2018 collection. On the mantel, a Roseville vase holds an uprooted magnolia tree. Antique ornaments adorn the branches. *Photography by Johanna Parker and J. P. d'Andrimont, courtesy Johanna Parker Design*

The white Christmas tree, from her mother's childhood home, is decorated with mercury glass beads and ornaments. It sits in a chartreuse McCoy pottery planter atop a mosaic tile-topped table. Beneath the tree are Johanna's collectibles and below the table are gifts wrapped in paper designed by Johanna.

The dining table is set for Christmas dinner with plates, napkins, and placemats designed by Johanna. The 1930s red Depression glassware belonged to her grandmother. A corner shelf is filled with pieces from Johanna's collections of vintage novelties and one-of-a-kind folk art sculptures.

Among keepsakes on the pottery shelf are Johanna's reproduction snowmen. Her Vintage Holiday Pennant Garland is printable, available from her website store.

Just inside the front door is a cabinet designed by Johanna and built by J. P. Her grandmother's turquoise vase holds Johanna's collection of vintage aluminum tree branches—its underside dripping with antique mercury glass baubles. The red velvet reindeer were her grandmother's. Walls in the entry are faux-painted in red and purple. Johanna painted the floral stems below the sconces.

The retro red tree on a kitchen cart sits in an old Fire King milk glass mixing bowl. On the refrigerator door hangs Johanna's design—a retro Waving Santa towel.

Johanna's studio is visible through the shaped archway with its crown of old bakelite spoons. Together J. P. and Johanna designed and built her unique workbench cabinet with custom art panels.

Moorish

Anzoategui Residence,
San Antonio, Texas
Karlos Anzoategui, Christmas décor

Karlos Anzoategui ("Karlos with a K," as his friends affectionately call him), has earned a reputation as "the host with the most." His home, Villa Sol, is a 1920s Moorish-style structure with Spanish revival elements. Its capacious rooms invite guests to mix and mingle during his popular summertime White Party and the glitzy New Year's Eve gala. For every event, large or small, Karlos dresses the villa (and himself) to the nines. He believes in the power of glitter and sparkle, especially for Christmas gatherings. "There is nothing traditional about my vision of Christmas décor—it's all about glamour," he says.

For Christmas 2017, he asked himself: "Wouldn't everyone want to find a Tiffany box under the tree?" Taking cues from the iconic blue box, he envisioned layers of aquamarine, turquoise, and forget-me-not blue for ornaments and decorations. Elements associated with Tiffany jewelry—sparkle, whimsy, and intricate detail—became part of the décor. Numerous objets d'art, many acquired at antique auctions, added his signature glamour.

Karlos executed his vision by layering swags of garland greenery and Tiffany-blue ribbon. He embellished the swags with glass ornaments, glitter-covered Tiffany-blue poinsettias, and berry branches, draping them over doorways, tabletops, and seating areas. Bowls filled with gold, silver, and Tiffany-blue ornaments graced side tables and the dining table.

Karlos is known for the extraordinary tablescapes he designs for chic dinner parties and informal soirees—not to mention the food. "I always include favorite comfort foods as well as exotic recipes from peoples who settled San Antonio over the past 300 years—Mexican, Spanish, English, German, Irish, and French," he says.

To Karlos, Christmas is about love and hope. "That's where I believe the power of glitter comes in. It transforms my villa into a magical, otherworld-like fantasy, encouraging others to believe that their dreams can come true," he says.

An eclectic gathering of exotic furnishings and decorations from around the globe are the background for soirees at the 1920s Moorish-style home of Karlos Anzoategui. *Photography by Waldinei Lafaitte*

A bowl of metallic fruit adds a holiday touch to a marble-topped coffee table laden with fascinating objects.

Tiffany's famed blue box inspired the Christmas decorating scheme, which included blue ribbon (for garlands), ornaments, faux blue poinsettias, and paint.

Karlos dressed for his annual Christmas party in a Tiffany-blue caftan, in keeping with the décor and theme.

For the dining table centerpiece, branches painted Tiffany blue add dramatic height and vivid contrast to silver and crystal sculptures, vases, and ornaments.

Merry

McClure Residence,
Wilmington, North Carolina
Debby Gomulka, interior designer

Debby Gomulka often decorates for clients with a theme in mind. One year it was a Charles Dickens Christmas featuring traditional reds and greens, another year a Marrakesh holiday with persimmon and sage green colors; one year the theme was a Hamptons Christmas in neutral tones.

Debby, an interior designer and adjunct professor of interior design at Cape Fear Community College, encourages clients to choose a color or two and then mix high and low, casual and dressy, and matte and shiny finishes.

For a holiday in the Hamptons, she imagined lace settings intertwined with pearl accents; placemats in a punchy green accented by raspberry-colored glassware and vintage crystal; gold and silver accessories, including stunning hammered silver platters with delicate gold-accented leaves; monogrammed linen napkins with red velvet trim and a jingle bell. In this scheme, she says, classic and trendy touches create a festive mood and a table setting that asks, "Won't you join me for Christmas dinner?"

To traditional interiors, she adds an element of surprise—vibrant color, luscious textures such as velvet and silk, and layered patterns. The result is what Debby calls "traditional with a twist." In one client's traditional home, she added layers of sparkle to create a festive mood and casual elegance. And on the classic veranda, visible through the dining room window, she placed boxwood in rustic copper urns, magnolia leaves, greenery, and a playful reindeer. Like many designers, she advocates collecting beautiful items from the garden and woods. "These collections will contribute to a fabulously decorated holiday home, one in which the eye will travel endlessly over wonderfully proportioned details, making new discoveries along the way," she says.

A sophisticated wreath with silver decorations adds glamour to the home of interior designer Debby Gomulko's client. *Photography by Cody Deer, courtesy Debby Gomulko Designs*

Needlepoint stockings at the mantel add a traditional touch to a highly eclectic interior, with its sophisticated mix of furniture and accessories. Sculptural white antlers are a striking focal point.

A bowl of ornaments underscore the moody blues of the oil paintings above a chest.

A pair of ice-skates beneath the flocked tree trimmed with her client's vintage decorations evoke nostalgic memories of former Michigan winters.

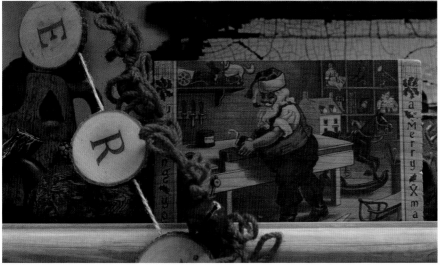

Red placemats strike a festive mood for a table set with Winter Greetings china. On the wall, a photograph of a red car with a Christmas tree on top lifts the holiday spirit.

A "Merry Christmas" greeting hangs on a shelf filled with art objects. Tucked behind the greeting is an antique image of Santa in his workshop.

Glorious

Blalock Residence,
Arlington, Virginia
Gloria de Lourdes Blalock, interior designer

The holiday tableau on her mantel is different each Christmas, but interior designer Gloria de Lourdes Blalock always includes her collectible golden peacocks. Surrounded by seasonal greenery and embellished with pinecones and other natural elements, the scene is a rich study in color and texture. Above the mantel, pussy willow stems and garden greenery are tucked behind the antique starburst mirror, which is backed by a thirty-inch metal frame with a rope edge. The effect is spectacular.

In the living room, twin mohair-covered sofas face each other across a coffee table, creating a cozy place for conversation with refreshments. The tall Christmas tree has its traditional space. "Ever since Breck and I purchased our home, the tree sits in this same cozy corner—to the rear of a sofa and visible from the front door and from both living and dining rooms," Gloria says. "We trim the tree with 1,200 lights and 800 treasured ornaments. The lights remain on from six a.m. until one a.m. The glow fills my heart with the joy of the season. The tree topper—a mirrored star—reminds me of the star that guided the Magi."

Gloria—a more-is-more maximalist—decorates her circa-1904 arts and crafts-style home to the nines for the holidays. "Our bungalow just feels like home when it's decorated," she says. She created a bar cart in the dining room, inspired by those she first saw in Europe as an exchange student. A mid-century bronze Don Juan sculpture sits on a ledge above the cart. "Given his legend, it's fitting that he guards the home libations," says Gloria. Throughout her home, she displays a collection of twenty English tea caddies. Atop one she places a Christmas-scene glass cloche.

On the dining table are candles in crystal holders. "I love candles," she says. "I burn dozens of tapers during the holiday season."

Gloria not only decorates her home, she decorates Summer, her fourteen-year old, four-footed shadow. "Summer wears a red velvet bow during the season. She's always camera-ready the entire month of December."

Pussy willow stems tucked behind the sunburst mirror add to its drama. On the mantel are golden peacocks from a collection. *Photography by Laura Sisino, courtesy Blalock Interiors, LLC*

A Christmas scene glass cloche sits atop an English tea caddy.

A real Christmas tree takes up its traditional position.

Roses adorning the dining table are symbols of energy and determination as Gloria engages in many new projects for the coming year.

Gloria's Christmas-spirits-filled bar cart in the dining room emulates those she first saw in Europe as an exchange student.

Christmas fairies in their holiday finery were gifts from long-time friend and photographer Laura Jens.

Gloria and her trusty pal, Summer, take a break—decorating is hard work!

INDEX OF DESIGNERS

Karlos Anzoatequi
Le Mirage,
555 Queen Anne Court
San Antonio, TX 78209
210-829-4142

Robert Baisch
Baisch & Skinner
2721 LaSalle Street
St. Louis, MO 63104
314-664-1212
www.BaischandSkinner.com

Mitzi Beach
Mitzi Beach Interiors
12 N. Cypress Drive
Wichita, KS 67205
316-686-4460
www.beboomersmart.com

Gloria de Lourdes Blalock
Blalock Interiors, LLC
1232 South Oakcrest Road
Arlington, VA 22202
703-969-8263
www.blalockinteriors.com

Mark Candelaria, AIA
Candelaria Design
6900 East Camelback Road, #400
Scottsdale, AZ 85251
602-604-2001
www.candelariadesign.com

Keith Carrington
7704 Martin Avenue
West Palm Beach, FL 33405
561-542-5381
www.KCDesignsPB.com

Shayla Copas, IDS
15 Hickory Hills Circle
Little Rock, AR 72212
501-258-7396
www.shaylacopas.com

Mary Douglas Drysdale
Drysdale, Inc.
2026 R Street, NW
Washington, DC 20009
202-588-0700
www.marydouglasdrysdale.com

Melissa Galt
Melissa Galt Interiors
4062 Peachtree Rd. NE, Suite A431
Brookhaven, GA 30319
404-788-6528
www.melissagaltinteriors.com

Debby Gomulka
Debby Gomulka Designs
412 Nun Street
Wilmington, NC 28401
910-352-7339
www.debbygomulkadesigns.com

Chris Hill, AIA
Gallagher Ranch
19179 S.H. 16
North Helotes, TX 78023
210-828-6565
www.gallagherheadquarters.com

Raven Labatt
254 Genesee Road
San Antonio, TX 78209
210-872-3402
www.ravenlabattinteriors.com

Tim Little
TX Luxury Interiors
PO Box 15001 Laurel Heights Station
San Antonio, TX 78212
210-663-7368
www.txluxuryinteriors.com

Patricia McLean
Patricia McLean Interiors, Inc.
3179 Maple Drive, Suite 10
Atlanta, GA 30350
404-266-9772
www.mcleaninteriors.com

Johanna Parker
Johanna Parker Design
8901 W. 20th Avenue
Lakewood, CO 80215
303-202-0203
www.johannaparkerdesign.com

Rhonda E. Peterson
Rhonda Peterson and Associates, LLC
7631 Broadhurst Drive
Riverdale, GA 30296
404-374-9662
www.rhondapeterson.com

Cheri Stith and Jamie Weyand
Feather, Fluff & Flings
219 Hillview Drive
San Antonio, TX 78209
210-860-7959
Featherfluffandflings.com

Leland Stone
Stone Standard
The Roosevelt Library
311 Roosevelt Avenue
San Antonio, TX 78210
210-862-10062
www.stonestandard.com
www.rooseveltlibrary.com

Marilyn Trainor Storey
MS Design Maven
395 Gardner Road
Marks, MS 38643
601-826-8470
www.msdesignmaven.com

Dustin Van Fleet
FUNK Living
309 E. 4th Street
Adel, GA 31620
229-520-7182
www.facebook.com/funkliving

Beth Webb
Beth Webb Interiors
425 Peachtree Hills Avenue, Suite
11-B-4
Atlanta, GA 30305
404-869-6367
www.beth@bethwebb.com

Howard Wiggins
233 Hearthstone Manor Lane
Brentwood, TN 37027
615-854-1468
www.howardwigginsinteriors.com